百鳥森林的音樂會

文／孟瑛如、林妙
圖／張瓊瑤
英文翻譯／吳侑達

在遙遠的深山裡，有一座美麗的森林。這個森林綠意盎然、古木參天，有許多奇珍異鳥齊聚在這裡，大家都稱這個森林為「百鳥森林」。

百鳥森林一年一度的「仲夏音樂會」即將到來。

黃鶯家族開始展開選角與集訓。

冠羽畫眉家族忙著整理華麗高聳的頭冠。

燕子家族則忙著銜乾草、花材、樹枝來布置音樂會的大舞台。

　　百鳥森林的鳥兒們都為了仲夏音樂會而忙碌，只有白鸛家族和烏鴉家族例外，這兩個家族從來就不會收到仲夏音樂會的邀請卡。

　　白鸛是百鳥森林中唯一不會發出聲音的鳥，他們是藉由上下嘴的急切敲擊來發出聲響。

　　烏鴉則是聲音沙啞低沉的鳥，在百鳥森林中，他們的歌聲從來就不受大家歡迎。

　　有一天，小白鸛樂樂在森林裡玩耍，飛著飛著，來到了仲夏音樂會的大舞台。樂樂從沒見過這樣漂亮的大舞台，他舞動雙翅，飛上飛下，東瞧瞧西探探，興奮得不得了！

　　樂ㄌㄜˋ樂ㄌㄜˋ回ㄏㄨㄟˊ到ㄉㄠˋ家ㄐㄧㄚ中ㄓㄨㄥ，指ㄓˇ著ㄓㄜ˙外ㄨㄞˋ面ㄇㄧㄢˋ的ㄉㄜ˙大ㄉㄚˋ舞ㄨˇ台ㄊㄞˊ，希ㄒㄧ望ㄨㄤˋ媽ㄇㄚ媽ㄇㄚ˙快ㄎㄨㄞˋ點ㄉㄧㄢˇ告ㄍㄠˋ訴ㄙㄨˋ他ㄊㄚ外ㄨㄞˋ面ㄇㄧㄢˋ在ㄗㄞˋ忙ㄇㄤˊ什ㄕㄣˊ麼ㄇㄜ˙。媽ㄇㄚ媽ㄇㄚ˙望ㄨㄤˋ著ㄓㄜ˙外ㄨㄞˋ頭ㄊㄡˊ，卻ㄑㄩㄝˋ只ㄓˇ是ㄕˋ長ㄔㄤˊ長ㄔㄤˊ的ㄉㄜ˙嘆ㄊㄢˋ了ㄌㄜ˙一ㄧˋ口ㄎㄡˇ氣ㄑㄧˋ。

　　樂ㄌㄜˋ樂ㄌㄜˋ不ㄅㄨˋ死ㄙˇ心ㄒㄧㄣ，衝ㄔㄨㄥ進ㄐㄧㄣˋ客ㄎㄜˋ廳ㄊㄧㄥ，急ㄐㄧˊ忙ㄇㄤˊ把ㄅㄚˇ爸ㄅㄚˋ爸ㄅㄚ˙拉ㄌㄚ到ㄉㄠˋ外ㄨㄞˋ頭ㄊㄡˊ瞧ㄑㄧㄠˊ瞧ㄑㄧㄠˊ。爸ㄅㄚˋ爸ㄅㄚ˙看ㄎㄢˋ著ㄓㄜ˙大ㄉㄚˋ舞ㄨˇ台ㄊㄞˊ，也ㄧㄝˇ只ㄓˇ是ㄕˋ拍ㄆㄞ一ㄧˋ拍ㄆㄞ樂ㄌㄜˋ樂ㄌㄜˋ的ㄉㄜ˙肩ㄐㄧㄢ膀ㄅㄤˇ，然ㄖㄢˊ後ㄏㄡˋ搖ㄧㄠˊ搖ㄧㄠˊ頭ㄊㄡˊ。

　　樂樂不解，為什麼爸爸媽媽的表情都如此奇怪？失望的樂樂就去找他的好朋友小烏鴉嘎嘎。嘎嘎正在午睡，睡眼惺忪的他被拉到森林的大舞台前。樂樂飛到華麗的大舞台中央翩翩起舞，彷彿自己是大明星，嘎嘎則在大舞台下，看著樂樂陶醉其中的模樣。

這時嘎嘎睡意全消，他把樂樂拉到角落小聲的說：「這是一年一度的森林音樂會，能夠上台的都是歌聲動人的家族。你們白鸛家族無法發出聲音，我們烏鴉家族則是聲音低沉沙啞不悅耳，所以我們兩個家族根本不會收到邀請函啦！」

　　嘎嘎說：「走走走，我們去別的地方玩吧！」這時，失望的樂樂根本提不起勁。

　　夜深了，大家都已經入睡，樂樂卻悶悶不樂的趴在窗台，呆呆的望著大舞台，心裡嘀咕著：「只剩兩天，仲夏音樂會就要開始了，為什麼我們家……」

　　正當樂樂嘀咕的時候，突然看到大舞台右側冒出一陣白煙，接著便聞到一股燒焦味。樂樂湊過去仔細一看，原來是天乾物燥，布置大舞台的乾草和枯枝起火了。

樂ㄌㄜ樂ㄌㄜ嚇ㄒㄧㄚ壞ㄏㄨㄞ了ㄌㄜ，趕ㄍㄢ緊ㄐㄧㄣ飛ㄈㄟ到ㄉㄠ屋ㄨ內ㄋㄟ，用ㄩㄥ嘴ㄗㄨㄟ大ㄉㄚ力ㄌㄧ敲ㄑㄧㄠ門ㄇㄣ，叫ㄐㄧㄠ醒ㄒㄧㄥ了ㄌㄜ爸ㄅㄚ爸ㄅㄚ媽ㄇㄚ媽ㄇㄚ和ㄏㄢ哥ㄍㄜ哥ㄍㄜ姐ㄐㄧㄝ姐ㄐㄧㄝ。

接ㄐㄧㄝ著ㄓㄜ，樂ㄌㄜ樂ㄌㄜ又ㄧㄡ飛ㄈㄟ去ㄑㄩ嘎ㄍㄚ嘎ㄍㄚ的ㄉㄜ家ㄐㄧㄚ，用ㄩㄥ他ㄊㄚ的ㄉㄜ嘴ㄗㄨㄟ猛ㄇㄥ烈ㄌㄧㄝ敲ㄑㄧㄠ地ㄉㄧ板ㄅㄢ，把ㄅㄚ嘎ㄍㄚ嘎ㄍㄚ一ㄧ家ㄐㄧㄚ都ㄉㄡ吵ㄔㄠ醒ㄒㄧㄥ了ㄌㄜ。

此時，白鸛家族用嘴奮力敲擊，發出巨大聲響，吵醒了百鳥森林所有的鳥兒們。

烏鴉家族則分頭大聲喊著：「失火啦！失火啦！大家快起來呀！」

於是，睡夢中的鳥兒們都被叫醒，大家齊力滅火，終於把大舞台的火撲滅了。但是，大舞台的華麗布置全都毀了，今年的仲夏音樂會也無法如期舉行了。

在滅火的過程中，有的鳥兒被濃煙嗆到，有的鳥兒羽毛被燻得焦黑，大家的樣子都很狼狽，不過還好大家都很平安。

　　因為被濃煙嗆到，黃鶯的聲音不再那麼嘹亮，黃鶯長老感慨的對烏鴉家族說：「你們的聲音雖然低沉沙啞，但是在那場大火中，卻是救命的關鍵啊！」

　　冠羽畫眉的冠羽被煙燻得凌
亂焦黑，他們也深刻體會到，
華麗高聳的頭冠在森林大火中
根本幫不上忙。所以他們慚愧
的對白鸛家族說：「謝謝你們
的奮力敲擊，發出那麼巨大的
聲響，才得以讓百鳥森林的鳥
兒們保住性命啊！」

於ㄩˊ是ㄕˋ，白ㄅㄞˊ鸛ㄍㄨㄢˋ家ㄐㄚ族ㄗㄨˊ和ㄏㄢˋ烏ㄨ鴉ㄧㄚ家ㄐㄚ族ㄗㄨˊ都ㄉㄡ收ㄕㄡ到ㄉㄠˋ了ㄌㄜ˙明ㄇㄧㄥˊ年ㄋㄧㄢˊ仲ㄓㄨㄥˋ夏ㄒㄧㄚˋ音ㄧㄣ樂ㄩㄝˋ會ㄏㄨㄟˋ的ㄉㄜ˙邀ㄧㄠ請ㄑㄧㄥˇ卡ㄎㄚˇ……

親愛的白鸛家族：

　　竭誠邀請您們加入明年仲夏音樂會的行列。

　　您們家族是天生的打擊樂手，敬邀擔任開幕典禮的開場節目嘉賓，期待您們精采的演出。

　　　　仲夏音樂會籌備會　敬邀

親愛的烏鴉家族：

　　竭誠邀請您們加入明年仲夏音樂會的行列。

　　您們家族是天生的節奏口技高手，敬邀擔任閉幕典禮的壓軸節目嘉賓，期待您們出色的表演。

　　　　仲夏音樂會籌備會　敬邀

給教師及家長的話

如果全世界的人都否定你，你是否還有信心做自己，繼續勇往直前呢？

《百鳥森林的音樂會》是描寫無法發出聲音的小白鸛樂樂，渴望參加百鳥森林仲夏音樂會的故事。白鸛家族無法發聲，只能靠著敲擊上下嘴出聲，而烏鴉家族雖然能夠發出聲音，但是音質沙啞不悅耳，所以百鳥森林的音樂會表演，這兩個家族從來不在受邀之列。小白鸛樂樂的個性積極樂觀，不想因為他人的既定印象而否定自己，一直懷抱夢想，期盼自己也能上大舞台表演。直到有一天，百鳥森林發生大火，這一場大火燒掉了華麗音樂會的虛無假象，終也將百鳥們對白鸛家族與烏鴉家族的成見化為灰燼；這一場大火點燃了百鳥們認識「天生我材必有用」的智慧之光，也照亮主角小白鸛「勇敢做自己」的追尋之路。

《百鳥森林的音樂會》故事的靈感是來自聽障者的溝通模式。故事中並未特別交代樂樂和嘎嘎是聽障或語障，畢竟聽障經常伴隨語障，且語障並非必然肇因於聽障。聽障者常被誤解為身處於「寂靜無聲的世界」，其實他們多數仍有殘存聽力，甚至非肇因於聽障的語障者在溝通過程，也可能需要手語的介入。不會發聲的小白鸛樂樂，擅長敲擊上下嘴及揮動羽翼，猶如使用手語的聽障者比手畫腳，手能生巧；小烏鴉嘎嘎能夠發出聲音但音質沙啞，就像有些慣用口語的聽障者，口雖能說卻不完全清晰。選擇音樂會作為故事背景，是想藉由歌聲悅耳的鳥兒們來烘托出唱歌對聽障者的困難。

配合《百鳥森林的音樂會》這個繪本故事，我們還另外編製了《百鳥森林的音樂會：學習手冊》，如果你是一般讀者，在讀完繪本後可以完成引導單 1-1 到 1-4 部分，此部分將有助於你更清楚故事結構與對文本的理解。如果想對聽覺障礙有更進一步的了解，或者你是聽障者本身、同儕、父母或老師，歡迎繼續完成引導單的後續部分。

《百鳥森林的音樂會》是否讓你看到了「勇氣」的可貴？是否喚醒你對每個生命體「尊重」的良知？至於《百鳥森林的音樂會：學習手冊》則期望能讓聽障學生認識並悅納自己、協助聽障學生的同儕能知道聽障者的身心特質與學習需求，並提醒聽障學生的父母與老師要找到孩子的亮點，以正向態度支持孩子。

「融合之愛系列」繪本與學習手冊乃眾人愛之融合，《百鳥森林的音樂會》繪本帶你邂逅「勇氣」與「尊重」，挺你「勇敢做自己」，進而「做最好的自己」。

註：《百鳥森林的音樂會：學習手冊》可單獨添購，每本定價新台幣 50 元，意者請洽本公司。

The Midsummer Concert in the Forest of A Hundred Birds

Written by Ying-Ru Meng & Miao Lin
Illustrated by Chiung-Yau Jang
Translated by Arik Wu

Deep in the remote mountains, there was a luxuriant forest where live all kinds of rare birds. The old trees in this forest were lush green and as tall as the sky. People called it "Forest of A Hundred Birds".

The Annual Midsummer Concert in the Forest of A Hundred Birds was drawing near.

The Oriole family started drafting and training their singers.

The Taiwan Yuhinas were busy fixing their tall, magnificent crested crowns.

The Swallow family was busy fetching hays, flowers, and sticks to decorate the main stage of the concert.

All birds in the Forest of A Hundred Birds were busy with the concert, except for the White Stork family and the Crow family. These two families never received an invitation to the concert.

White storks were the only bird that did not sing in the forest. They only made loud sounds by clattering their bills swiftly.

Crows, on the other hand, were only able to make hoarse noises. Their voice, as a result, was never appreciated in the Forest of A Hundred Birds.

One day, Le Le, a little white stork, was playing around in the forest. He flew hither and thither, accidentally arrived at the main stage of the Midsummer Concert.

Le Le had never seen a stage as grand as this. He flapped his wings in excitement, flying up and down to survey it.

After Le Le went back home, he pointed at the huge stage outside in hopes that his mom would tell him what was going on out there. However, his mom just looked outside the window and took a long sigh.

Le Le did not give up. He dragged his dad outside to see the stage, but his dad just gave him a pat on his shoulder, and shook his head.

Le Le was so confused. Why were mom and dad so weird? Disappointed, he went looking for his best friend Ga Ga, a little crow. Ga Ga looked very sleepy when Le Le dragged him to see the grand main stage, because he just woke up from his afternoon nap. As soon as they arrived, Le Le flew up to the main stage and started dancing as if he was a super star.

Ga Ga's sleepiness was gone immediately. He whispered in Le Le's ear, "This is the stage for the Annual Midsummer Concert. Only those who sing beautifully are invited! You white storks can't even sing, and we crows only make hoarse noises... we are never on the list!"

"Come on! Let us go play somewhere else." Ga Ga said. However, Le Le was too disappointed to summon up the momentum to do so...

The night had come, and the entire White Stork family was sound asleep, except for Le Le. He leaned against the windowsill and gazed at the main stage outside. He murmured in his mind, "Only two days left for the Midsummer Concert... why weren't we invited..."

While he was murmuring, he suddenly saw a column of smoke rising from the right side of the main stage. Then he smelled something burning. Le Le leaned forward to take a closer look. It turned out that it was the sticks and hays that were used to decorate the stage were on fire, due to the dry and hot weather.

Le Le was so terrified. He flew back to the house and knocked on the door with his bills, woke up his parents, brothers, and sisters.

Then he flew to Ga Ga's house and smacked the floor with his bills, woke up the entire Crow family.

The white storks started clattering their bills at the same time, making loud noises to wake up every single bird in the forest.

Meanwhile, the crows were flying around the forest crying, "The stage is on fire! Wake up! Wake up!"

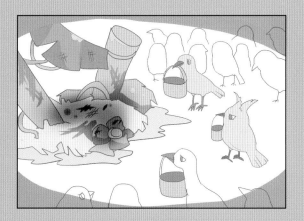

The white storks and the crows woke every single bird up, and together they put out the fire. But the grand decoration was all gone—there was no way that the Midsummer Concert this year would be held on time.

During putting out the conflagration, some birds were choked by the thick smoke, and some had their feathers singed. Everyone looked terrible, but thankfully they were all safe and sound.

The orioles' voices were not as loud and beautiful as they were before, due to the smoke they inhaled. The elder in the Oriole family said to the crow with mixed emotions, "Although your voice is hoarse... it saved our lives last night."

The Taiwan Yuhinas also had their crested crowns singed. It had finally dawned on them how useless their tall, magnificent crested crowns were during a forest fire. They said ashamedly to the white storks, "If it were not for your clattering and loud sounds, birds in our forest would not be saved!"

As a result, both the White Stork family and the Crow family received an invitation to the Midsummer Concert the next year...

Dear White Stork family,
    We cordially invite you to attend the Midsummer Concert next year and would be honored if you would perform in the opening ceremony.
    You are born to be great percussionists, and we look forward to your performance.

            Sincerely yours,
    The Preparatory Committee
    for the Midsummer Concert

Dear Crow family,
    We cordially invite you to attend the Midsummer Concert next year and would be honored if you would perform in the closing ceremony.
    You are born to be great beatbox players, and we look forward to your performance.

            Sincerely yours,
    The Preparatory Committee
    for the Midsummer Concert